Pausing
with
Purpose

ENDORSEMENTS

" "**L**ent is a time to reflect and remember the passion, death, and resurrection of our Savior and Redeemer. As you prepare for the celebration of Easter Sunday, I would encourage you to pick up the devotional, *Pausing With Purpose* by C.J. Vegter. This is a wonderful forty-day devotional to keep you mindful of His love and sacrifice for us. The short but probing daily devotions will call you into a deeper walk with Jesus and keep you focused on the meaning of Lent and Easter."

SHAREN BREWER, WOMEN'S LEADER

Hope Church, Bentonville, AR

" "**I**n a day where our lives are constantly bombarded by distractions, *Pausing With Purpose* offers relief as a refreshing, short, daily tool that guides readers into a deeper relationship with Christ. Writer C.J. Vegter takes you on a journey of growth using real-life experience and deep life-changing quotes that the Lord has revealed to her through life. Her humble and transparent authenticity connects powerfully with any reader. I've known C.J. for many years and have seen her dedication to the Lord firsthand. When I faced trials, she consistently helped me to focus on the Lord and His purposes. She now shares this life-giving attitude to benefit anyone who wants to walk through life's struggles as a victor!"

JEFF MCINTOSH, KIDZ PASTOR

Cross Assembly, Raleigh, NC

" "**A** very easy and concise read. C.J's ability to shift our thinking where it needs to be—during Lent or any time of the year—is most excellent. Each day's devotional thought provokes the reader to press in and reflect on their own journey with the Lord. Her ability to share relational stories ties the theme and scriptural reference together quite nicely. Giving the reader the opportunity to journal with our own take-aways and prayers is a great bonus! Thank-you, C.J., for being vulnerable and transparent as you share your gifts with us. Loved it!"

JIM AND WENDY PAISLEY, YOUTH PASTORS
St. Augustine, FL

"A perfect Lenten companion, *Pausing with Purpose: A Lenten Devotional* offers personal stories, interactive sections, chapter summaries, and closing prayers. Deepen your relationship with Jesus and embrace personal transformation in this beautifully written devotional. A must-read for spiritual growth during Lent."

PAUL DURBIN, PASTOR
Belay Church, Boulder, CO
Author of *When Jesus Stole My Bread*

"C.J. Vegter's Lenten devotional is inspiring and encouraging. Each day's reading includes a deeply personal and, usually, humble story from C.J.'s life or an evocative passage from the Scriptures. These allow the reader to lower shame-based, self-protective mechanisms, which are usually derived from some sort of trauma. This enables us to fearlessly acknowledge our stumbles and grow stronger by inviting the Holy Spirit to heal, empower, and motivate us to be who God intended. One unusual thing about C.J.'s writing is that the reader can relate to the heart of her message, even though we may not have shared her particular circumstances.

The art of her prose is realism, not abstraction. Thus, the Lord connects to us through her in very practical and applicable ways!"

Dr. Mike Tenneson
Department Chair and Professor of Biology
Evangel University, Springfield, MO

"This was an uplifting daily read during the season of Lent (or any season). C.J. takes Scripture, the story of Jesus, and her personal journey and ties them together in a beautiful way."

Heidi Dennis, MS, LPC
Therapist, Speaker, and Author of *Hello, Anxiety*
Bentonville, AR

"Refreshing for the soul! I'd be privileged to weigh in and encourage folks to take to heart the devotional offerings of C.J. Vegter. C.J. brings a positive, faith-filled word with insight and creativity. I am always encouraged in the Lord after each read! 'Taste and see that the Lord is good' (Psalm 34:8)!"

Wanda Talley
Retired missionary
Memphis, TN

Pausing
with
Purpose

A LENTEN DEVOTIONAL

C.J. VEGTER

AMBASSADOR INTERNATIONAL
GREENVILLE, SOUTH CAROLINA & BELFAST, NORTHERN IRELAND

www.ambassador-international.com

PAUSING WITH PURPOSE

A Lenten Devotional

Hardcover ISBN: 978-1-64960-431-6

Paperback ISBN: 978-1-64960-696-9

eISBN: 978-1-64960-479-8

Cover design by Karen Slayne

Interior typesetting by Dentelle Design

Edited by Katie Cruice Smith and Kate Marlett

Scripture quotations are taken from the *The Holy Bible,* English Standard Version. ESV® Text Edition: 2016. Copyright © 2001 by Crossway Bibles, a publishing ministry of Good News Publishers.

Ambassador International books may be purchased in bulk for education, business, fundraising, or sales promotional use. For information, please email sales@emeraldhouse.com.

AMBASSADOR INTERNATIONAL
Emerald House
411 University Ridge, Suite B14
Greenville, SC 29601
United States
www.ambassador-international.com

AMBASSADOR BOOKS
The Mount
2 Woodstock Link
Belfast, BT6 8DD
Northern Ireland, United Kingdom
www.ambassadormedia.co.uk

The colophon is a trademark of Ambassador, a Christian publishing company.

To my family,

who diligently and faithfully walked me through this journey of healing.

TABLE OF CONTENTS

Delay is not denial—not even withholding. It is the opportunity for God to work out your problems and accomplish your desires in the most wonderful way possible for you.[1]

---

1   Two Listeners, *God's Calling*, A.J. Russell, ed. (Pasadena: Hope Publishing House, 2012).

Author's Note

Dear Friend,

I am imagining that we are sitting down daily with this devotional over a cup of coffee or hot steamer (my favorite), discussing each of our journeys with Jesus. Right now, I want to share my side of the story; and I hope if you enjoy this devotional, you will reach out to me and share your side. I left space for you as a reader to journal after each devotional and prayer.

When I started these quotes in 2010, it was a challenge to wake up every day and think of something profound but spiritual. I originally posted them on social media for years until God wanted me to add more to it. Through God healing my body from Lyme disease, alphagal syndrome, and food allergies, I found hope in these quotes that renewed my walk with Christ. It was not an instant healing, and it was a journey that I would never wish on anyone. However, I still would not trade it. From pain, we grow, and we learn on *Whom* we need to lean. Christ is my Rock; and when darkness came—sometimes for many days—He would carry me on His shoulders like a Shepherd carrying His lost sheep back home.

I also wrote this devotional to help others find their hope in Jesus as their Rock and Shepherd. The world is full of struggles and discouraging voices, and I want this devotional to be a light that helps point you back to Jesus—our Healer, our Salvation, and our Hope.

Many of these devotionals were written years ago when I was in the middle of some of the worst days of my chronic disease. But I can testify to you right now that I am completely healed! God has healed my alpha-gal syndrome, other food allergies, and my Lyme disease. I want to testify that God is still healing people on this earth. God used what Satan meant to distract and harm me to help write this devotional to testify about God's healing touch and to encourage you as a reader to not give up. Healing will come!

C.J. VEGTER

Day 1

*"And being found in human form, he humbled himself by becoming
obedient to the point of death, even death on a cross."*

Philippians 2:8

*Giving up something is not the focus of this season; recognizing that
Jesus gave up all for us should be our focus.*

It is so easy to focus inward during this season of Lent. When
you tell yourself that you need to give up something, it becomes
the topic of conversations—and your life—for the next forty days.
"Giving up" has a purpose to it. It should not be about how we can
handle the sacrifice; it is about joining in Christ's sufferings, even
if we cannot completely understand His sufferings. So, this means
we should be thinking of Christ every time we miss that "thing" we
have sacrificed.

This whole season should be a realigning of our focus on Christ.
It could mean giving up or adding a new spiritual habit to our lives.
One year, God asked me to thank Him each time I was experiencing
chronic pain that limited my movements or activities. It was not easy,
but it helped deepen my relationship with Jesus and lessen my pain.

17

What is God asking you to refocus in your life? What distractions are you allowing to take your eyes off Jesus?

Prayer: Lord, help me to keep my eyes fixed on You and show me the areas of my life that need to be refocused. Amen.

NOTES

_____

_____

_____

_____

_____

_____

_____

_____

_____

_____

_____

_____

_____

_____

_____

_____

_____

_____

_____

DAY 2

"God is spirit, and those who worship him must worship in spirit and truth."

John 4:24

Worship is not just lifting our hands in a song; it is our heart's cry to praise God in everything we do!

What do you think when you hear the word "worship"? I initially think of music and songs that I know or sing a lot, but that is not the only thing worship is. Living a life of worship is letting God be involved in everything you do. He is not Someone we just talk to once a week or when we need help. He wants to be a part of our whole day.

For example, when my daughter was three, she had a variety of imaginary friends; but she also had Jesus as a real Friend. She probably did not even know the meaning of worship, but in her innocence, she understood that Jesus wanted to be a part of her life. During Christmas, she would get really close to "Baby Jesus" in the manger and talk quietly to him. Knowing that she did not learn that from us, we realized it must have just come from the heart of worship inside of her.

Where is Jesus during your day-to-day activities? What is your "heart of worship"?

Prayer: Lord, I want my heart of worship to be involved in every moment of my life. Help me to let You into my daily activities, so I can be a witness to others for You. Amen.

NOTES

_____

_____

_____

_____

_____

_____

_____

_____

_____

_____

_____

_____

_____

_____

_____

_____

_____

DAY 3

"The Spirit of God has made me, and the breath of the Almighty gives me life."

Job 33:4

If it is true that we came from dust and will return to dust (Gen. 3:19), then what makes us special? Only the breath of God makes us unique!

We breathe in just over two thousand gallons of air a day to help oxygenate our blood so that the blood can take it to the body. The tissues and organs would fail without oxygen, and the wrong kind of air would make us suffocate.[2]

Spiritually, that is true, too; we need to keep breathing in the Spirit of God to keep our temple of the Holy Spirit working. God took extra time in creating the exact specifications of the Israelites' tabernacle and temple. How much more important are we since we now are the temple of the Holy Spirit? Spending time in His presence by prayer, Scripture meditation, and accountability with other believers is key to getting the breath of God in us.

---

2   "How Your Lungs Get the Job Done," American Lung Association, July 20, 2017. https://www.lung.org/blog/how-your-lungs-work.

What area do you need to work on during this season to help get the breath of God moving through you? Remember, the more you breathe in His breath, the more your uniqueness shines through!

Prayer: Lord, I love how You created me. Please help me be able to show others how You created them special, too.

NOTES

_____

_____

_____

_____

_____

_____

_____

_____

_____

_____

_____

_____

_____

_____

_____

_____

_____

_____

DAY 4

*"And let steadfastness have its full effect, that you may be perfect and
complete, lacking in nothing."*

James 1:4

*Life is full of choices, whether good or bad. It is important to choose
to learn from the past and keep moving forward.*

Growing up overseas, most restaurants or grocery stores
had few options; so when we came back to the States, my
family was always overwhelmed by how many options we had at
restaurants, stores, and malls. One time, my mom told me to go
choose my own box of cereal. I was excited to finally get to pick
my own breakfast; but when I got to the cereal aisle, I froze. There
were too many options!

In our spiritual lives, we are bombarded with so many options,
like what church to go to, what Bible version to use, and what
devotional to read, among others. At one point during my health
journey, I kept flip-flopping on a medical choice in my life and could
not get peace. God finally told me, "Either one is fine; I will be there
with you in both." That was when I realized that God does care what

we choose. Most of the time, He wants us to take a step of faith. Then He will continually guide us forward from that step.

What choice are you struggling with today—your kid's education, finances, job options, etc.? Sometimes, the past haunts us when trying to make future decisions. Today, let us practice letting go of the worry that we will make the wrong choice and trust God with our choices.

Prayer: Lord, help me to make the most important choice of following You this morning and help give me wisdom and peace about all the choices I make today. Amen.

NOTES

_____

_____

_____

_____

_____

_____

_____

_____

_____

_____

_____

_____

_____

_____

DAY 5

*"So the men took some of their provisions, but did not ask counsel
from the LORD."*

Joshua 9:14

*How different our lives might be if we "inquire of the Lord" more
often!*

In Joshua 9, Joshua and the Israelites were extremely feared by surrounding tribes of people. A tribe pretended to be from a far-off land to make a treaty with them. Joshua was leery, but the rest were fooled. Still, the leaders signed a treaty with a neighboring tribe. The Israelites chose not to ask God before they partook in what they made for them. Instead, the Israelites probably lost the territory that God had planned for them to have.

How many times should we consult the Lord before we do something but do not? I am not saying that every decision—like whether to turn right or left—should always be asked of God, but maybe sometimes, we should. During this season of Lent, spend more time asking for wisdom about decisions, whether it is in work relationships, friendships, family decisions, finances, or anything else. I know I could use all the wisdom God will give, even in daily decisions.

What stops you from asking God for help? Do you feel too small in God's eyes for Him to care about your little problem? God cares about the big and little details of our lives. Remember what Jesus said: "Are not two sparrows sold for a penny? And not one of them will fall to the ground apart from your Father. But even the hairs of your head are all numbered. Fear not, therefore; you are of more value than many sparrows" (Matt. 10:29-31).

Prayer: Jesus, help me ask for help, even in the small details of my life. Help me inquire of You, Lord, more often. Amen.

NOTES

_____

_____

_____

_____

_____

_____

_____

_____

_____

_____

_____

_____

_____

DAY 6

"Jesus said to him, 'No one who puts his hand to the plow and looks back is fit for the kingdom of God.'"

Luke 9:62

It is not about looking back at past failures or accomplishments. It is about what the future can be because of our past.

My main love language is words of affirmation, so encouraging statements are always something I crave to hear. But I take criticism very hard. For example, I used to work as a tour guide for a theme park. All day long, I kept getting compliments on how great my tours were; but on the last tour of the day, a couple complained. Sadly, I finished that day of work only dwelling on the negative comment when, in truth, all the positive comments should have outweighed the one negative one.

Why is it so easy to hold on to the negative instead of the positive words? I still look at my past mistakes and can easily beat myself up over what I have done wrong. How can we take captive those negative thoughts? How can we not let past mistakes define us but change us for the future?

One verse I often quote to help retrain my perspective and words is Philippians 4:8: "Finally, brothers, whatever is true, whatever is honorable, whatever is just, whatever is pure, whatever is lovely, whatever is commendable, if there is any excellence, if there is anything worthy of praise, think about these things." During this season of Lent, we should focus on how we can change the future by learning from the negatives and turning them into a positive change in our minds and lives.

Prayer: Jesus, help me keep my eyes on You. Thank You for forgiving my mistakes. I need Your help in letting go of the negative thoughts and words in my life. Thank You for providing me with guidance for the future. Amen.

NOTES

_____

_____

_____

_____

_____

_____

_____

_____

_____

_____

_____

_____

_____

DAY 7

"And the vessel he was making of clay was spoiled in the potter's hand, and he reworked it into another vessel, as it seemed good to the potter to do."

Jeremiah 18:4

I pray that You shape me for Your glory so that when I close my eyes I see Your face!

Making pottery is all about patience and detail. The one time I got to make my own pottery dish, I used the coil technique, which was making a bowl while coiling clay around and around into different designs. I noticed I had to keep my hands and clay wet with water to be able to mold the clay better. I learned that the potter can never leave the clay during its forming process.

This is also true with God. When He is working us into His vessel, He gets His hands dirty by feeling our pain during this process. He knows what we are going through. He feels the ups and downs in the forming process and is right there next to us through it all.

In the end, the pottery must be fired to be made into a strong and beautiful piece. There have been times in life I felt like I was in the fire, and you might be going through the same thing. I had to remind myself that the fire was going to make me stronger and that my Creator was with me the whole time.

Are you in the fire right now? Are you feeling the molding going on in your life? Do not forget He forms each pot of clay specially and is there with each of us until completion. He knows every groove He has created, and that is what makes us special and truly created by His hand.

Prayer: Lord, thank You for getting Your hands dirty when You are molding me. Help me rest that You are with me during this difficult season and give me a glimpse of the finished product You are working on. Amen.

NOTES

_____

_____

_____

_____

_____

_____

_____

_____

_____

_____

_____

_____

_____

DAY 8

*"The steadfast love of the LORD never ceases; his mercies never come
to an end; they are new every morning; great is your faithfulness."*
Lamentations 3:22-23

*Focusing only on what you have already missed will make you miss
new blessings for today and the future.*

I am a very slow reader, which makes reading books like the Bible
very hard for me. I struggle each day to make sure I read, but guilt
takes over most days. I keep feeling like I am not good enough to be
a child of God because I forget to read my Bible, which is all lies from
Satan. He just wants me to be distracted from feeling God's mercy
and grace every day.

So, how can we make each day a new beginning? How many
things do we carry with us each day that are not ours to carry? We
need to follow Jesus' example. In Mark 1:35, Jesus got up early, found
a quiet place, and prayed. Recently, I have been trying to do the same;
since it is dark outside, I get the pleasure of just staring at the stars
and listening to Scripture. I mentally let go of my worries and let
them rise to the stars.

Looking up at the stars and planets reminds me that the Creator of the universe Who keeps us in orbit also cares about us personally. When we have messed up and asked for forgiveness, God is merciful to us and forgives us. If we do not forgive ourselves, it is just a trick of Satan trying to steal our joy. We *cannot* allow that.

This season of Lent is a time of preparation for Jesus' sacrifice, where He paid the *whole* price for our sins. Make it a daily reminder that we are forgiven and free from the past. Holding on to the past only hurts our Father's heart.

Prayer: Jesus, I need Your help to accept Your forgiveness. Help me see Your mercies every morning and give myself a fresh start. Amen.

NOTES

_____

_____

_____

_____

_____

_____

_____

_____

_____

_____

_____

_____

_____

DAY 9

"Behold, I stand at the door and knock. If anyone hears my voice and opens the door, I will come in to him and eat with him, and he with me."

Revelation 3:20

God loves hearing from us, no matter what we are going through.

Soon after my daughter was born, we noticed she did not eat or defecate well. Many people said she was colicky, but I kept thinking there was something more. Hearing doctors say she would grow out of it was not helpful when I was just trying to make it through each day. As we searched for answers, I heard God speak to me through many setbacks and sleepless nights. I finally learned to hone in on His voice over all the other voices.

I felt the Lord telling me to fast and pray. The first week I started fasting, God sent me a lovely mom who had a son with a rare condition that made him allergic to a lot of food and outside allergens. She listened to me many times when I was so frustrated with the doctors and had no answers. Slowly, we started getting answers during that month of fasting and praying, but the answers were not only from the doctors—they were from God, too. I remember while sweeping the floors, God spoke to me about changing all my daughter's cookware and dishes. When I did, it made a huge difference. Now I can show my daughter that God healed her.

Remember whatever struggle you are going through during this Lent season, keep talking to God. Are you feeling discouraged? Are you overwhelmed by the trials and troubles you are facing? Jesus said in John 16:33b, "'In the world you will have tribulation. But take heart; I have overcome the world.'"

Prayer: Lord, keep reminding me that You have overcome the world. Help me to be still and listen when the world seems to be collapsing around me. Also, give me hope through these struggles I am facing. Amen.

NOTES

_____

_____

_____

_____

_____

_____

_____

_____

_____

_____

_____

_____

_____

_____

DAY 10

"For 'everyone who calls on the name of the Lord will be saved.'"

Romans 10:13

When we're spiritually out of gas and stalled out, whom do we call to the rescue?

My husband fixes computers in an IT department, and one scenario plays out over and over again. Someone will be having an issue with their computer; and despite all their best efforts, they cannot solve the problem. As soon as they call my husband or show up at his desk, however, the computer magically works. The same thing can happen in our relationship with God. We are so stressed and worried about health issues, financial struggles, or family concerns. Still, we try to fix it in our own ways. We even go to others to ask for advice. Then after all those avenues fail, we go to God.

Why do we not go to God first? Why do we not spend quiet time with Him, listening and talking to Him about our mountain? He can guide us to ask for advice from a specific person, or He might tell us in a still, small voice what we need to know. He might even just want us to rest in His presence in this fast-paced world in which we live.

Today, take a moment and go to God first. Ask Him for guidance and peace about whatever situation or mountain you are facing. God can move the mountain; but if He does not, He definitely can help you over it or guide you on the best path to around it.

Prayer: Jesus, whether You move the mountain or not, it is in my path to help me keep my eyes on You and call on Your Name first. Thank You for letting us call You any time, any day. Amen.

NOTES

_____

_____

_____

_____

_____

_____

_____

_____

_____

_____

_____

_____

_____

_____

_____

_____

DAY 11

*A step of faith does not always give immediate results but always
brings long-term benefits.*

In 2010, I was excited about my upcoming trip to Spain. I thought the trip was going to all be about my next step in ministry, but it took an unexpected turn. During our meal times, I noticed a cute guy at the retreat always wearing a yellow shirt. All week, I never had a chance to figure out who he was. But finally, on the last day, I ran into him in the hotel lobby.

I boldly went up to him and asked, "Who are you?"

Even though we only chatted for ten minutes, a connection was made. As he was leaving, I was disappointed I had not had the chance to meet this cute guy earlier.

Later, before my flight home, I got onto Facebook, took a leap of faith, and added him as a friend. A couple days later, I got my first message from him, which I found out later was a leap of faith for him, too. We were married in October 2011; and after all these years, he still has that same "lucky" yellow shirt.

Are you in a place where you are cautious to take the next step? Have past experiences made you leery of giving your complete trust in God?

Prayer: Lord, I know that faith is the assurance of things hoped for. Help me to continue to have hope in Your direction and encourage me to be brave enough to step out in faith for things I have not even seen yet. Amen.

NOTES

_____

_____

_____

_____

_____

_____

_____

_____

_____

_____

_____

_____

_____

_____

_____

DAY 12

"Oil and perfume make the heart glad, and the sweetness of a friend comes from his earnest counsel."

Proverbs 27:9

Lifelong friends are like full moons; you do not always get to enjoy them every day, but you know they are still there.

I have been blessed with many friends all over the world. Some, I talk to a couple of times a week; and others, it might be longer. But when we do talk, it is always like old times. God has blessed us with the need for community. Thankfully, friendships are what we can take to Heaven. Community within the body of Christ is key.

In Luke 5:17-26, four friends helped lower their paralyzed friend to Jesus. That is a true sign of friendship; knowing that their sick friend could not do it for himself, they became a support team for him to receive his healing.

Since I became sick, I read this passage much differently than before. I have been blessed with many teammates who have figuratively carried me to Jesus in prayer during my rough times. That is exactly what the body of Christ is supposed to do. Friendship and community are about praying together, listening to each other, crying on each other's shoulders, and laughing together. If you have these kinds of friends, make sure you thank them for their support. If you are struggling to find those kinds of friends, pray that God will bring the right people in your life. Also, remember that you will be the support they need when the time comes.

Who is a friend you could reach out to and thank? Is there someone who needs encouragement today?

Prayer: Jesus, You know the feeling of losing friends, but You were extremely great at being a Friend. Teach me how to be a great friend and bring the right people in my life that can be my support and accountability. Amen.

NOTES

_____

_____

_____

_____

_____

_____

_____

_____

_____

_____

_____

_____

_____

DAY 13

"Wait for the LORD; be strong, and let your heart take courage;
wait for the LORD!"

Psalm 27:14

Waiting for what the heart wants will always bring greater reward
than instant gratification.

None of us like to wait. We do not want to wait in long lines, so we find the shortest one. We do not like to wait in traffic, so we leave early or find a different route. We especially do not like to wait for God's answers.

I feel like my time as a single adult was the longest waiting period. I really wanted to be married, but it was not happening. At one point, I thought I was dating the perfect guy and believed we were going to be married; but he decided he did not want marriage. I was truly heartbroken but knew it was the right decision for us both. It would still be a few more years till I met my husband, but God had to do some healing and molding in my life before then.

Waiting stinks, especially when you do not know what you are waiting for. Are you in a holding pattern in your life? Do you feel like this waiting time has no purpose? Today, when you are faced with a waiting situation, thank God for the wait. You never know what God has protected you from during that waiting season.

Prayer: Father God, You know I dislike the waiting, but I know You see the bigger picture. Help me have peace in the waiting. Amen.

NOTES

_____

_____

_____

_____

_____

_____

_____

_____

_____

_____

_____

_____

_____

_____

_____

_____

_____

_____

DAY 14

"Come to me, all who labor and are heavy laden, and I will give you rest."

Matthew 11:28

True rest is found in the healing and loving arms of our Savior.

Ⓘ grew up in South America; and the Latin culture is very slow-paced, focusing on family and community. Because of this, my personality is more community-orientated than time-focused. Since moving back to the States in my twenties, I started focusing on what I accomplished during the day rather than on relationships. It was not until I got sick with Lyme disease that everything about my life had to slow down. I quickly learned that there are seasons, maybe even years, of needed sabbatical rest.

Even though I am getting better, I still cannot do the same amount of activities as others, which I believe God has allowed. Rest is key for my healing. God has even put a day of rest into the week for all of us to use. Do you use this day like God designed it? Rest is hard when the world around us is still moving. During this season of Lent, ask yourself if you are taking a day of rest. If this word has never been in your vocabulary or lifestyle, then pray that God can show you how.

Prayer: God, I am sorry I haven't been good at taking a real rest. I need Your help to slow down. Help me to find time in my day to rest mentally, spiritually, and physically. Amen.

NOTES

_____

_____

_____

_____

_____

_____

_____

_____

_____

_____

_____

_____

_____

_____

_____

_____

_____

_____

DAY 15

"But he said to me, 'My grace is sufficient for you, for my power is made perfect in weakness.' Therefore I will boast all the more gladly of my weaknesses, so that the power of Christ may rest upon me."

2 Corinthians 12:9

If God's strength is made perfect through our weakness, then, Lord, help me to admit my weakness so You can shine through me.

Do you ever feel stumped when a job interviewer asks what your weaknesses are? It feels like they are intentionally trying to find something that you cannot do so that they have a reason not to hire you. My husband conducts job interviews for his job and explains that question better. It is not about their weakness; it is about how the person can show themselves working through their weakness.

It is so easy in life to focus on our strengths and even boast about them, but what if we boasted about our weaknesses? That would be embarrassing! I think the point that Paul is making in 2 Corinthians is to point out who gets the glory. Are we making sure God gets the glory in our weakness and strengths?

For example, I flew so much when I was growing up that it was easy and I loved it; but when I moved to Thailand, things changed. I was on my way back to the States for a trip, and I had an anxiety attack on the flight. After that, I still flew a lot, but it was always a struggle to set foot on each plane. I asked God why He allowed this to happen, and He whispered to my heart, "Before you depended on yourself to travel; now, you have to depend on Me."

What weakness do you hide from others because you are embarrassed by it? Are you depending solely on yourself in certain areas? Today, let's pray that God uses your weakness to let His light shine through you.

Prayer: Father God, my weaknesses are hard to admit, but I know that You can help me be stronger if I let You take control. Show me the areas where I have not given You full control. Amen.

NOTES

_____

_____

_____

_____

_____

_____

_____

_____

_____

_____

DAY 16

"But now, O LORD, you are our Father; we are the clay,
and you are our potter; we are all the work of your hand."

Isaiah 64:8

If we are clay and He is the Potter, then remember that each time He
molds us, He leaves His fingerprints on us.

When the word *molding* comes to mind, I think of getting a massage. Our bodies naturally get tight and stiff; and sometimes, we need a massage to break apart the knots and help relax the muscles that have been overused or injured. Spiritually, we need massages, too. We might need to let God massage the knots out of us. It definitely will hurt, but it will make us stronger and ready for the next adventure.

During a Bible study, I remember using a piece of clay as an object lesson. While I molded it, I noticed that each time I moved the clay with my fingers, I left a clear mark on the clay of my fingerprints. It reminded me of when God molds us. How comforting it is to know that each time God molds us, we can see more of God's handprint in our lives. Nobody wants to go through hurt or pain; but if we allow God's hand on our lives, His fingerprint will be visible to others.

What situation are you not letting God mold you? Are you afraid of the pain that will be worked out of you? Pain is only temporary when you become a better vessel for God to use for His kingdom.

Prayer: Father God, please show me areas that I need to let You mold in me. When I am afraid, help me trust You have the finished product in mind. Amen.

NOTES

_____

_____

_____

_____

_____

_____

_____

_____

_____

_____

_____

_____

_____

_____

_____

DAY 17

"For God gave us a spirit not of fear but of power and love and self-control."

2 Timothy 1:7

Warning: Fear is a choking hazard.

When I felt the Lord wanted me to start writing these little quotes in 2010, I had this horrible dream where I was being choked by a demon. I could not see him, but I could feel myself being choked. Finally, I rebuked him in the name of Jesus; he let go, and I woke up. That is when I realized fear chokes us; it chokes our dreams, our passions, and our relationships. When we let fear control our thoughts, choices, and lives, it chokes us from living in the truth God has provided.

Even now, when I think about writing, I get scared. I question myself, "Will it make a difference? Will anyone read it?" But that is only fear speaking. It does not matter what others think in the long run. Are you called to something that scares you? Have you been dragging your feet because you feel like you are not equipped for the task?

Before I moved to Thailand, I was told, "God doesn't call the equipped; He equips the called!" If God has called you to do something, you cannot let fear get in the way. Sometimes, a small step of faith every day is what it takes to follow God's calling for your life.

Prayer: Jesus, I know You have called me. I need to know what steps I need to take to fulfill what You have called me to do. Amen.

NOTES

_____

_____

_____

_____

_____

_____

_____

_____

_____

_____

_____

_____

_____

_____

_____

_____

_____

_____

_____

Day 18

"And the peace of God, which surpasses all understanding,
will guard your hearts and your minds in Christ Jesus."

Philippians 4:7

Emotions need not be the principal driver, only to be a passenger on
our road trip of life.

Women tend to be placed in the category of being "emotional." In truth, everyone has emotions; it is part of how God created us. My emotions can be affected by many things, such as hormones, relationships, and sleep deprivation. No one said emotions were bad, but letting them rule our decisions can hurt us and others. The question is how do we let ourselves have emotions without us being controlled by them?

I usually recite Philippians 4:7 as a prayer over people; but after reading it through the eyes of emotions, it sounds so different. God wants to give us peace, even with our emotional journey of life. He can guard our hearts when emotional hurt suddenly happens. He can guard our minds when emotional words bruise us. There will always be hurt, pain, and frustration in this life; but we need to let God help us navigate through these emotions.

I remember while dating Mark, I felt like I was on a roller coaster of emotions. *Will he text me, or should I? Will he call or not?* But each time I went to God and prayed about the relationship, I always got a sense of peace deep down that I could not explain. During the time we dated long-distance, God used my relationship with Mark to help heal past hurts in my life. It was not an easy season, but it made me a better woman for Mark to marry.

Are you struggling with emotional ups and downs? Has something happened to make you let your emotions lead you? Has hurt kept you from giving your life to Christ?

Prayer: Jesus, I need You. My emotions are a battle each day. I have been hurt so much that it is hard to let You lead my life. Help me let You lead instead of letting my emotions rule. Amen.

NOTES

_____

_____

_____

_____

_____

_____

_____

_____

_____

_____

DAY 19

"For the righteous falls seven times and rises again,
but the wicked stumble in times of calamity."

Proverbs 24:16

Failures will come, but they are not the end result. They are only the
means to learn how to do it better for the next time.

One of my favorite quotes from the book *In a Pit with a Lion on a Snowy Day* by Mark Batterson is, "He wants to recycle your adversity and turn it into a ministry."[3] How many of us love to fail? I am assuming not many. Failure seems so final, even in our finite minds. But what if the failure had to be accomplished so that the right victory could come to pass?

In college, some of the classes were easy for me because of the training I got in high school, but I finally had a class that hit me hard. I did horribly on my first test; and since the grade was mainly based on the test scores, I knew at this rate that I was going to fail the class. The way he taught and gave tests was different from any of

---

3   Mark Batterson, *In a Pit with a Lion on a Snowy Day: How to Survive and Thrive When Opportunity Roars* (Colorado Springs: Multnomah, 2016).

my previous experiences. I had to change my studying habits. Even though he allowed a "cheat sheet" during tests, it was not helpful for me. I had to make flashcards of all the vocabulary in the chapters and memorize them. Soon, I started seeing a difference in my test scores. The failure made me change the way I looked at the problem.

What kind of problem are you facing today? Do you need to have a failure to help you be stronger and better for the next time? If we do have a failure, we do not need to be afraid because God is walking with us at each step.

Prayer: God, failure is hard, but I know that You are teaching me something from it. Help me see the purpose in the falls and praise You when I rise again. Amen.

NOTES

_____

_____

_____

_____

_____

_____

_____

_____

_____

_____

_____

_____

_____

DAY 20

"Keep steady my steps according to your promise,
and let no iniquity get dominion over me."

Psalm 119:133

Following Jesus does not always make sense right now, but right now
is not what we are supposed to be living for.

About a month before I was to graduate college, my plans to go to nursing school did not work out. I was hurt at first because I had no idea what I was going to do next. Even though I went through the emotions of disappointment, I still had peace about my future. Weeks before this happened, God whispered to me that "something was coming." He did not tell me what, but I knew something was about to change.

Even after the disappointing news of nursing school, I kept moving forward with some ideas of what to do next; but honestly, I was open to anything. One of my best friends came and visited me during my searching time and introduced me to a missionary family from Thailand. I told the wife my whole story.

Afterward, she looked at me and said, "Do you want to come to Thailand and work?"

Right then, I knew that was it. One door had closed, but another one had opened. Within two months after graduation, I was on a plane to Bangkok, Thailand, for a two-year assignment.

We do not always see the next steps in life when we are following Jesus, but faith is a huge part of this journey. Taking steps of faith never makes earthly sense, but they make heavenly sense. What steps of faith do you need to take right now? Are you willing to grab Jesus' hand and step out?

Prayer: Jesus, it is so easy to focus on the unanswered prayers. Help me rest in the hope that You are guiding my steps, even though I might not see the whole path. Amen.

NOTES

_____

_____

_____

_____

_____

_____

_____

_____

_____

_____

_____

DAY 21

"'Blessed are those who mourn, for they shall be comforted.'"

Matthew 5:4

The tears of sorrow water the seeds of new life.

Life is not fair. Life hurts, but new life brings joy. New life brings hope. I do not know many mothers who say they had non-painful contractions when giving birth. Through the pain of childbirth comes a new life of a precious baby.

I had a scary birthing experience, but the best moment was when the nurses came to me asking me what I predicted my baby's gender to be. I had all along predicted I was having a boy; but to my surprise, I had a baby girl. That surprise was such a joyful blessing after everything that had happened.

There are always going to be sorrow and struggles in our lives. How can we use our tears from those struggles and sorrows to help plant new life? I have been blessed that through my continuous struggle with Lyme disease and chronic pain, God has used me to comfort others through their chronic pain and suffering. I also have helped people find the right doctor to help them get better. I never thought that my story of pain would be the story I write about the most, but God truly takes what was meant for bad and turns it into something good.

Are you discouraged by your continuous suffering? Is the pain too heavy to carry? Today, try to embrace the suffering and sorrow. Even be bold enough to thank God for it because He is always there to comfort you through it.

Prayer: Father God, I am thanking You for this struggle, but I believe that one day, I will be healed. It might not be healing this side of Heaven, but I trust that You are going to use this for a greater good. Thank You for always being by my side during this journey. Amen.

NOTES

_____

_____

_____

_____

_____

_____

_____

_____

_____

_____

_____

_____

_____

_____

Day 22

"Be still, and know that I am God."

Psalm 46:10a

Quiet your soul and listen to the inner workings of His Spirit. When confusion and frustration come, rest on the stillness and peace of the answers God gives you.

Many couples debate the difference between listening and hearing. "To listen" means to take notice of and act on what someone says; "to hear" means only to perceive with the ear the sound made by someone or something. I know my husband does hear me, but sometimes, there are too many distractions for him to listen to me.

After I became sick, I struggled with my communication. If there are too many things for my brain to hear, it would shut down into a brain fog moment. My thoughts would just stay in my head; when I would try to say something, nothing would happen. I hated these moments because I felt like I was in slow motion and the world around me was going at superspeed.

Since I have had these experiences, it has made me slow down and focus on my listening. Before I became sick, I was in a fast-paced lifestyle, trying to do two jobs and be a mom, all while my husband was working full time and being a full-time graduate student. No one wants to say that my sickness was a good thing; but now, I appreciate it in hindsight. I am glad my life had to slow down. Being still has always been hard for me. I loved being busy, but making sure I have "still" moments is so important to my health physically and spiritually.

Listening to God's voice is hard when we have so many ways of hearing things from social media, T.V., and friends. None of those are bad, but they can easily drown out God's voice. Are you able to hear God's voice? Do you find it hard to make time to be still? It might be hard the first time to have a quiet moment with God, but the more you do it, the easier it will get.

Prayer: God, I know that slowing down is key to my spiritual, mental, and physical health. Help me slow down and be a more active listener to Your voice. Amen.

NOTES

_____

_____

_____

_____

_____

_____

_____

_____

_____

_____

DAY 23

"Therefore, since we are surrounded by so great a cloud of witnesses, let us also lay aside every weight, and sin which clings so closely, and let us run with endurance the race that is set before us."

Hebrews 12:1

As every racetrack has perimeters guiding the racers for a faster and safer race, God has perimeters in our race to help us reach the finish line strong!

An Olympian race comes to mind when I read that Scripture. The runners always start out in their own lanes; but after the shot rings out for the start of the race, they all go to the inner lane. It is a shorter distance in the inner circle. You can still race on the far edge of the track, but it will take you longer than others.

Do I sometimes not know my own parameters that God has set for me? Am I putting in parameters that God does not want there? I know I have sometimes made this harder for myself than it needed to be. I struggle with perfectionism and getting it done right. I want to look, sound, and act in the correct way. I want others to notice my improvements and accomplishments. Posting my achievements on social media is not all bad; but if the "likes" and comments are what I live for, it could make the race a lot harder and longer when trying to reach the finish line.

Salvation is grace-driven. If we are always trying to work for our salvation, we will fail. The inner circle is much quicker in our race; and for me, this means we need to draw closer to Jesus on this race. Jesus wants to help us during the race.

Are you focusing on the world watching you or on the race itself? Are you trying to keep up with the perfection that others expect? Even if the world does not take notice to what I do, I need to remember that I should be obedient to what God is asking me to do.

Prayer: Lord, You have mapped this race out for me, and I know You are here to guide me. Help me to trust You and to keep my eyes on You instead of the crowds all around me. I want to be in the inner circle closer to You, Jesus. Amen.

NOTES

_____

_____

_____

_____

_____

_____

_____

_____

_____

DAY 24

"Do not quench the Spirit."

1 Thessalonians 5:19

As wax melts by burning fire, I pray that my heart melts for the world by the fire of the Holy Spirit.

During the first year of my sickness, one of my best friends came into town to help and encourage me. We heard a quote by Charles Spurgeon that quickened my spirit: "The sun shines out of the heavens upon wax and softens it, but at the same time it shines upon clay and hardens it."[4] I realized that there will be both kinds of people that I try to witness to or pray with. For some, their hearts will just get harder; but for others, they will melt right away.

I can see similar situations with my own heart. I have let my heart harden to daily sights like street beggars or even talking with my neighbors. I might see worldwide issues and cry; but when it comes to day-to-day life, I do not let the Holy Spirit move me as I

4   Charles Haddon Spurgeon, "The Heart of Flesh," *Metropolitan Tabernacle Pulpit 19* (Kansas City: The Spurgeon Center, 1873), https://www.spurgeon.org/resource-library/sermons/the-heart-of-flesh/#flipbook.

should. Why do I do that? Maybe I am embarrassed or care too much about what others think about me. What about you? Are you letting your heart harden?

Prayer: Lord, change my heart so that it melts for everyone and help me to actively listen to the nudging of the Holy Spirit when You speak. Amen.

NOTES

_____

_____

_____

_____

_____

_____

_____

_____

_____

_____

_____

_____

_____

_____

_____

_____

_____

_____

DAY 25

"Put on the whole armor of God, that you may be able to stand against the schemes of the devil."

Ephesians 6:11

If a soldier would never leave home without his armor, then what makes us think we can leave home without the armor of God?

Nobody wants to acknowledge that there is a war going on—a spiritual war. Peace is what all people seem to want in the world today. I cannot deny that peace is a wonderful idea; and one day, in a new world, we can have peace. As for right now, it is impossible to have true peace without Jesus. Still, even if we have peace, we will still encounter trouble because we have a spiritual enemy that is against us and against anything God wants to accomplish through us. Our battle is daily; and sometimes, it is so easy to forget about it because we either ignore it or do not want to "over-spiritualize" life.

The truth is all of life is both equally physical and spiritual—but do not misunderstand me. Every bad thing that happens during the day is not necessarily of the devil. Think about Sunday mornings. How many of us either want an extra hour of sleep or have more fights with our family before trying to make it to church? The enemy does not want us to have a community that is uplifting and encouraging to our faith. The enemy wants to tear God's church apart, and He is doing it in small, hidden ways. That is why it is so important to have on the armor of God. We need to guard our minds and hearts with the armor of God. We need to combat the enemy's lies by never losing hope in meeting together with other believers, meditating on Scripture, and praying. God has given us tools such as Scripture, community, and prayer to protect ourselves in this spiritual war. Have you found yourself forgetting that even with this spiritual battle, we have God on our side? Have you tried to fix issues and problems by yourself?

Prayer: Jesus, I know that the battle is Yours. I know You are the Victor in the end and in my life today. But I sometimes choose to walk outside without the armor You have equipped me with. Help me remember that "Your word is a lamp to my feet and a light to my path"5 and that spending time with You will make me a stronger fighter. Amen.

NOTES

_____

_____

_____

_____

_____

_____

_____

_____

5   Psalm 119:105

DAY 26

"And the Lord said: 'Because this people draw near with their mouth and honor me with their lips, while their hearts are far from me, and their fear of me is a commandment taught by men.'"

Isaiah 29:13

Worshipping God just with your voice is not enough.
He wants our heart of worship.

In a Bible study group I was in, another member mentioned that she started writing out Scripture instead of just reading it. I felt challenged that day to start doing that myself. I cannot say that I have done it every day; but when I do, I have noticed how I pay more attention to the words that are in the passage I am writing. I sometimes have to re-read the paragraph to make sure I did not miss any words or skip a line. Slowing down and writing the words of Scripture makes me see small things that I might easily pass over with a quick read.

Do we not do the same with songs that we sing in the car or at home? It does not matter what song we sing; if we have sung it too much, we usually forget the words we are saying. Today, take your favorite worship song and write down the lyrics. Make them your prayer and anthem for the day.

Prayer: Jesus, You are my Anthem. I sing to You from deep in my heart. You are my worship. Amen.

NOTES

_____

_____

_____

_____

_____

_____

_____

_____

_____

_____

_____

_____

_____

_____

_____

_____

_____

_____

DAY 27

"For you formed my inward parts; you knitted me together in my mother's womb. I praise you, for I am fearfully and wonderfully made. Wonderful are your works; my soul knows it very well."

Psalm 139:13-14

With a world full of many different people, let's not focus on our differences but on the fact that we are all loved equally by God!

Our differences need to be celebrated! We are all created uniquely by God, but what makes us all the same is that God loves us equally. Our society does too much comparing. People get awards for comparing one movie or song with another. Some get "likes" because we are comparing one post or tweet as better than another. We are human, and our flaw is that we cannot stop comparing ourselves. I am sure that will not change anytime soon, but the one thing we should *never* compare with others is how much God loves each of us.

He sent His Son to die for *all* of us—not for just one elite group or a super spiritual group. He came to die for each one of us. That love that God has for us is so grand that we probably cannot comprehend it. Are you willing to die for a family member? Probably! Are you willing to die for a stranger or even an enemy? Probably not. But Jesus died for His enemies *and* His friends. That is a lot of love. Are you struggling to love someone today? Are you struggling to feel love by others or by Jesus?

Prayer: Jesus, You have unconditional love. You made the ultimate sacrifice. Help me first to feel Your love in my life. Also help me love others in the same way You love me. Amen.

NOTES

_____

_____

_____

_____

_____

_____

_____

_____

_____

_____

_____

_____

_____

_____

_____

_____

_____

DAY 28

"For my thoughts are not your thoughts, neither are your ways my ways,
declares the LORD. For as the heavens are higher than the earth, so are
my ways higher than your ways and my thoughts than your thoughts."

Isaiah 55:8-9

When the puzzle pieces of life do not seem to fit together, take a look
at who is trying to make things fit. Is it God or us?

Looking and applying for jobs have always happened a bit differently for me. Many times, God has asked me to take a step of faith and quit a job before the next one was even close to sight. I am not advising this for everyone—it just is how God has worked in my life.

When I needed to decide to leave Thailand, I had no idea where I would go or what I would do next. But at the first job fair I went to in the States, I got a job offer immediately. Even though this is how God works in my life, I would still try to do things on my own.

There was a time period when I was applying for jobs online and would not stop. Then I clearly heard God tell me that was enough. That week, I ended up finding out I had shingles. I had no energy to even try looking for jobs. During that week of rest, I got offered a job and had an interview the next week. Once again, God proved to me that things are better when He is in control. So many times, when I try to put all the pieces together, I fail miserably; but when I let God take control of the pieces of my life, miracles happen. Has it been hard to let go of control in certain areas of your life? What kind of things do you need to give back to God?

Prayer: Father God, I know I have a tendency to try to put life's puzzle pieces together by myself. I usually mess up, but I know that You can help me. Please help me give these pieces of my life back to You to take control. Amen.

NOTES

_____

_____

_____

_____

_____

_____

_____

_____

_____

_____

_____

_____

_____

DAY 29

*"As for you, you meant evil against me, but God meant it for good, to
bring it about that many people should be kept alive, as they are today."*

Genesis 50:20

*Counting our blessings is not just about counting the good things; it
is also counting the painful things, knowing that God can turn them
into something better.*

When I wrote this statement in 2010, I probably was dealing
with the emotional pain of past relationships and the journey
of being single, but I never would have guessed what the pain would
mean to me later. Counting my chronic pain as a blessing is something
I do not want to do.

In 2017, during the season of Lent, God asked me to thank Him
whenever my chronic pain flared up. I cannot say it was easy or if
it helped my pain go away, but it gave me a more positive outlook.
Thanking God for the gifts He has given us is easy, but thanking Him
for the rough times is hard.

God allowed Joseph to go through what he did because there was
a bigger purpose for him. Thankfully, Joseph did not lose hope. No

one would blame him if he did. I might not know what the bigger picture is for this chronic disease, but I can tell you now that my compassion for others has changed a lot. I have also been blessed to help others through their own struggles with food allergies, Lyme disease, and alpha-gal syndrome.

Are you in the midst of a storm? Has pain—emotional, mental, or physical—overwhelmed you? Do not give up hope! We all have our struggles, and each of us has different ones. But even when we cannot see the light at the end of the tunnel, God is going to use that struggle for a purpose.

Prayer: God, I am worn out. I keep facing these struggles; and even when things do get better, I am still faced with pain. I know there is a purpose to this struggle. Help me be grateful for the pain. Give me hope that the one day, this pain will end in Your perfect world. Amen.

NOTES

_____

_____

_____

_____

_____

_____

_____

_____

_____

_____

Day 30

"For as by the one man's disobedience the many were made sinners,
so by the one man's obedience the many will be made righteous."

Romans 5:19

"What do I owe God?" I owe God more than I could ever repay.
That fact alone should shape how I live my life.

What first comes to mind when you hear, "What do I owe?" I think of paying back for something that was bought for me or lent to me. One fall, a group of ladies from church went on a trip to Kansas City; but something came up, and I could not go. I was so looking forward to many parts of the trip, but one thing was that I could go to a certain grocery store to get unsweetened mango slices for my husband. I honestly cannot remember if I mentioned the mango slices to anyone, but one of my friends brought me back a few packages of them, to which I was thrilled! She handed them to me as I was getting ready to teach children's church, and I totally forgot to ask what I owed. I did finally ask her a few days later, and she graciously said, "Nothing." Such a blessing!

But our mindset as humans is that we naturally have this feeling we owe people something for what they give or do for us. Nothing seems free, unless you wait in a line for a long time to get it or you save coupons for it; and even then, you have had to give your time. Salvation being free is such a rare concept and hard to accept. Do we owe God? Yes! We do owe Him. His Son, Jesus, died for us, paying the price we could never pay. If we always look at our salvation as something we must pay back, we will work our whole lives and never pay back what Jesus did for us.

Prayer: God, You sent Your Son to die for me. That is a huge sacrifice. There are times I feel like I need to pay You back for Your gift, but I know I cannot. Help me seek You and Your presence over trying to work for my salvation. Amen.

NOTES

_____

_____

_____

_____

_____

_____

_____

_____

_____

_____

_____

_____

_____

_____

DAY 31

"But I have trusted in your steadfast love;
my heart shall rejoice in your salvation."

Psalm 13:5

The flower of love needs to be rooted deep in the soil of trust for it to
continue to grow and bud into more flowers of love!

As humans, we make mistakes. We hurt others intentionally or unintentionally; and each time we get hurt, we are less likely to trust the next person we meet. Trust is something that gets built over time.

Moving a lot as a missionary kid made it easy for me to make friends, but the hard part was building deep friendships. Sometimes, I struggled to trust; and other times, I trusted too quickly. I got hurt, and it made me wary of building long-term friendships. Thankfully, over time, I did.

Trusting God is hard, too. When you do not see the end results or what is going to happen next, it is difficult to trust God. The moments we stop trusting God, we forget about His love, too. A while back, there was a time I did not feel God's love. I served Him and loved

Him but felt so far away from Him. I even tried to read books to help me. He was always still there loving me, but the real issue was I was looking for love from a boyfriend.

At that time, I loved the guy more than he liked me. The relationship was so unbalanced, but I did not know that at the time. Things did not really get better; but finally, my eyes were not blinded by my infatuation anymore. He was not a horrible guy; it was just an unbalanced relationship. I thank God that I learned a lot from that and realized my love and trust needed to be first in God alone before my other relationships. Even now, after marriage to the great husband God has provided for me, I can easily go to my husband for love and dependence when I should first be going to God for those things. My husband can never fill me the way God can.

Do you have an unbalanced relationship? Do you struggle feeling unloved by God? Are you thinking your works will be what gets others and God to love you?

Prayer: Lord Jesus, I need to know that You complete me. Help me find fulfillment in You today. Also, if there are any unbalanced relationships in my life, please show them to me and help me make them balanced. Amen.

NOTES

_____

_____

_____

_____

_____

_____

DAY 32

"Remember not the former things, nor consider the things of old. Behold, I am doing a new thing; now it springs forth, do you not perceive it? I will make a way in the wilderness and rivers in the desert."

Isaiah 43:18-19

When God closes a chapter in your book of life, trying to reopen it or rewrite it will only delay the beginning of a new chapter that God wants to start with you.

Spring is almost here. I see some of the flowers blooming and some grass creeping out in midst of the dead grass. Thinking of spring brings the idea that there is a chance for something new to come. What might have died or looked dead in the winter can come back with a new bud of life in the spring. Sometimes on our journeys, we want to be done with the chapter in our life because of all the pain and heartache that went with it. Other times, we have had such a great chapter, we do not want to let go of that seemingly perfect life. Each time, God usually does exactly the opposite of what we want.

When the chapter on pain will not close, it is probably because He is going to use the pain for His good purpose. When God closes a productive, happy chapter, it might be because He is preparing you for a new adventure, where there could be struggles. But He knows the strength He helped you build in the last chapter will help you through the next one. My main purpose is to say that with whatever dies, new life always comes from it. Jesus had to die to rise from the grave. He had to die with all our sins, so we all might have new life in Him.

Is there a chapter in your life you do not want to close? Or is there a chapter in your life that you are desperate to be done?

Prayer: Jesus, thank You for dying for my sins! Thank You for showing me that from death comes new life. Help me understand what that means in my day-to-day routine. Amen.

NOTES

_____

_____

_____

_____

_____

_____

_____

_____

_____

_____

_____

_____

_____

DAY 33

"Therefore you also must be ready, for the Son the Man is coming at an hour you do not expect."

Matthew 24:44

Live like Jesus is coming today; plan like He is coming in one hundred years.

I waited all week to tell my daughter her best friend was coming to visit. My strategy worked until the morning of their arrival. As soon as I told her, she ran upstairs and stared out our bedroom window, expecting them to arrive. It did not matter what I told her; all she heard was her best friend was coming.

Is that how God wants us to be? From what Scripture says, my answer is yes. Still, God knows we need to work and plan wisely. But is that true, even if our work and future plans take our eyes off our Savior? Too often, I get so bogged down with the mundane that I forget that we need to be expecting His return. How do we get ready and not get caught sitting at the window waiting all day?

When my daughter returned, disappointed, I suggested making a card or a coloring page for her friend's arrival. That is when it hit me—being ready for Jesus' return is about our priorities. There are millions of things around us that can fill our days and distract us. Am I making time to listen, talk, rest, and spend time with Jesus? The more I spend time with Him, the readier I am for His return. Can I turn mundane things into service for my Savior? Can I take time today to listen to Jesus?

Prayer: Jesus, help me be ready for Your return by spending more time with You. Help me incorporate praying and reading the Bible into my busy life as a daily practice. Amen.

NOTES

_____

_____

_____

_____

_____

_____

_____

_____

_____

_____

_____

_____

_____

_____

_____

_____

DAY 34

*"See what kind of love the Father has given to us, that we should be
called children of God; and so we are. The reason why the world does
not know us is that it did not know him."*

1 John 3:1

*Never believe what people "perceive" about you because it is what
God sees in you that is important.*

What do people think of me? Am I a cool mom, wife, or woman? Do I work hard enough? Do I disappoint others with my actions? These are all questions that often run through my head. I hate to admit that I do care about what people think of me. I am a people-pleaser. I want to make others happy, but the truth is that I cannot make everyone happy. I will disappoint others, but what I need to practice daily is that I am ultimately serving God.

Even still, I struggle with thoughts of what others think of me. I so badly want to look good in others' eyes. What has made me care about people's perceptions of me? I think we all do care about what people think. If your boss is happy with your work, you could be promoted; but if he is displeased, you could lose your job. If your family and friends like their gifts, you might finally have a deeper connection with them; but if they do not like the gift, you could get the cold shoulder. These might be extreme cases, but they are real situations just the same.

Each day, I need to keep reminding myself that no matter what, I need to primarily care about what God thinks of me over others. He created me. He loves me. He believes in me. He knows me better than I know myself. Maybe the world cannot forgive our mistakes easily, but God can. Are you struggling with those questions of worthiness? Do you feel like you are not enough?

Prayer: Lord Jesus, please come and remind me You see me as Your child. You love me deeply because You created me. Help me block out what others think of me and only focus on what You think of me. Thank You for always loving me. Amen.

NOTES

_____

_____

_____

_____

_____

_____

_____

_____

_____

_____

_____

DAY 35

"Rejoice in hope, be patient in tribulation, be constant in prayer."

Romans 12:12

With the world full of girls looking for their prince, there has always been a Prince of Peace waiting patiently and lovingly for them.

It might look from an outsider that I can say this phrase easily because I am married to a wonderful man, but I wrote this phrase when I was twenty-seven years old and single. By this point, I had met a handful of great guys, but I clearly remember God saying no each time I prayed about them. It was not easy having God say no or not yet. But during this time, God was trying to form me into His daughter. He wanted me to long for Him as I longed for a husband.

In February of 2010, before Lent season had started, God gave me a promise through an unexpected song. At that time, Michael Bublé's song "Haven't Met You Yet" came out, and that phrase was God's promise to me. I held onto that promise, always trusting and believing that God was going to surprise me, no matter when it was going to happen.

Soon after, God challenged me to write these phrases that are in this devotional. I had a sense that something was coming and that God was preparing me for an adventure. At the time, I thought it was for the mission field, but I was wrong. About a month or so after Easter, I met Mark. I had no idea God was preparing me to meet my husband.

Are you in the stage of life where you are longing to meet your significant other? Please do not give up hope. Are you struggling to be patient?

Prayer: Jesus, thank You for the surprises You have in store for me. Help me to be patient and keep forming me into the person You want me to be for whatever adventure You have in store for me. Amen.

NOTES

_____

_____

_____

_____

_____

_____

_____

_____

_____

_____

_____

_____

_____

DAY 36

"And let us run with endurance the race that is set before us, looking to Jesus, the founder and perfecter of our faith."

Hebrews 12:1b-2a

As we drive, distractions come that take our eyes off the road. We need to make sure that the distractions of life do not take our eyes off Jesus.

One of my first symptoms when I got sick was dizziness. The dizziness would come on suddenly, and it took a long time for my brain to get back to normal. It was hard to describe to doctors because it felt like I could not focus on what I was looking at. I would close my eyes and then open them, trying to focus; but most of the time, it would not work. Later on, I learned that I have a glitch in my brain that changes my level of eyesight higher up and to the left than what is normal. This is why driving—especially on highways with cars and buildings passing by quickly—made my dizziness worse. Outside distractions were my worst enemy until I got my prism glasses to help balance my sight back to normal.

As Christ's followers, there are various distractions on our journey. It is easy to let distractions like worry, pain, money, or even good things keep us from our race. Think about when you first learned how to drive. Your hands gripped the steering wheel, and your eyes focused on the road ahead. The more you drive, the easier it gets to ignore basic distractions; but then, there are always new distractions that we must train ourselves to ignore. Keeping our eyes on the road is still true in real life and in our spiritual walk. Not all distractions are bad, but it is letting them lead in our life and journey that is harmful.

Are the distractions of this world overwhelming? Are you letting worry, money, or pain distract you? Do you have fellow believers who can hold you accountable when you get off your path?

Prayer: Dear Jesus, I need Your help. I cannot do this journey You have placed me on without You. Please help put friends in my life who can hold me accountable. Help me not be distracted by the worries of this world. Help me to keep my eyes fixed on You, Jesus! Amen.

NOTES

_____

_____

_____

_____

_____

_____

_____

_____

_____

_____

DAY 37

"For still the vision awaits its appointed time; it hastens to the end—it will not lie. If it seems slow, wait for it; it will surely come; it will not delay."

Habakkuk 2:3

It is not about whether God can heal us or not; it is about if we can trust in His timing so He gets the glory and not us!

Reading this statement I wrote years ago is even truer today than it was back then. I know very well that I feel better today than I did two years ago or even a year ago; but when I have bad days, I still wonder how long I will have to battle this disease. After reading this, I know that God is in control. He will not delay! He is faithful.

I have so many dreams for my family and myself, but many of them must be placed on the backburner for another day. Even though I do not have an exact date for when that day will happen, I do know that through this slow process of healing, God will always get the glory. He has opened doors for me to see doctors very quickly when the waiting list has been over six months' long. He has provided the right support groups around me to encourage me through the roughest days. He has given me wisdom about what to do next when doctors do not have any answers. God has truly been the ultimate Doctor through all this; and though I have not been instantly healed, I know that God is with me through the rough days and the good days.

Are you struggling with a chronic disease, an unknown diagnosis, or anything that seems to never end? Do not give up hope! You might not see it now, but God is working through you. And a miracle will come of this that you can testify about later. Is healing not coming as you thought? Remember, the best hope we have is that we will be completely and fully healed in Heaven!

Prayer: Thank You, God, that every day You blessed me with what I have on earth, You constantly remind me that this is just temporary. Thank You for making a place in Heaven that is painless! Amen.

NOTES

_____

_____

_____

_____

_____

_____

_____

_____

_____

_____

_____

DAY 38

"No one word of all the good promises that the LORD had made to the house of Israel had failed; all came to pass."

Joshua 21:45

We doubt God because of the unfulfilled promises for the future when He wants to remind us of His fulfilled promises of the past.

The Israelites easily forgot all that God did for them. He parted the Red Sea and gave them food and water every day; but when Moses was gone for too long, they gave up and made an idol to worship. When I read their actions in the Scriptures, it is easy for me to judge them; but I do that, too, do I not? How many things has God provided for my family and me over and over again, but I still question if He will keep His promises? Why do I do that?

As soon as we get the promotion, we start looking for something bigger and better. Our lives are surrounded by discontentment. I do not want to treat God like a genie or a wish machine because He is way more than that. My prayer today is that I continue to be content with what God has blessed me with—even the small things. I never want to take for granted the little miracles that happen each day.

Are you complaining about what God has not done yet? Are you not grateful for the past promises that God has kept? Then it is time to do some introspection and remember what He has done.

Prayer: Father God, thank You first for the answers to prayer You have done over the years of my life. Thank You for not failing on Your promises. Help me to put my hope in You. Keep reminding me of the fulfilled promises of the past when I become doubtful of future promises. Amen.

NOTES

_____

_____

_____

_____

_____

_____

_____

_____

_____

_____

_____

_____

_____

_____

_____

_____

DAY 39

"Every branch in me that does not bear fruit he takes away, and every branch that does bear fruit he prunes, that it may bear more fruit."

John 15:2

As a bush needs to be pruned to remove unhealthy parts, we need to be pruned, too. Although it hurts and leaves a scar, we will grow stronger and healthier after the pruning.

Every scar has a story. Some are too painful, while others are a reminder that we are survivors. Before I met my husband, I had another relationship that quickly turned serious. I was so in love with him that I did not see what was really happening. Our eventual breakup was difficult and still not public for various reasons.

My mom, to whom I always talk about everything, was recovering from hip surgery. I was alone in the hurt and anger. I was grateful that God brought a friend via online messaging to talk to me and encourage me through those days. When I returned to my mother to help in her recovery, we found out that my maternal grandma had passed away. Since my mom could not go to the funeral, my dad went instead. That whole week of emotions was stuffed far down deep inside me. I really did not deal with them because they hurt so badly. It was not until I met Mark that God started bringing back my insecurities. Since Mark and I were long-distance, I started to have flashbacks to my previous relationship.

I asked God one day, "Why are You bringing this junk up?"

His response was, "You never dealt with it properly."

He used my relationship with Mark as a healing process for me to bandage the scar I had left. God had to get out the bad infection that was leaving me angry and bitter so that I could flourish and heal with this new relationship. It was painful and rough to fight through those insecurities, but I know that is where the healing began.

Do you have some anger and bitterness in your life? Have you not dealt with some past hurts? God wants to prune them out of your life. Ask God for His help.

Prayer: Jesus, I know that there are things in my past that I might not have dealt with properly. There has been some hurt and unforgiveness in my life. Please help me forgive others like You have forgiven me, even if they do not see their wrongdoing. I need Your help to move forward and to heal. Amen.

NOTES

_____

_____

_____

_____

_____

DAY 40

"From the rising of the sun to its setting,
the name of the LORD is to be praised!"

Psalm 113:3

The sun rises on everyone; the beauty of it is determined by the eye
of the beholder.

My mom always said sunlight was the best light to put on makeup. I would definitely agree. Have you ever tried putting makeup on in the dark? I have. It ends up a disaster. We need good light; and sometimes, the best light is the sun. The sun does show imperfections in our skin, but it also shows the details of our faces.

I need the sun to point out the imperfections that I have allowed to hide in the dark rooms of my life. We all have secrets, and some of them are hard to open up about because we do not want to be judged or looked down on by others. But God wants us to confess our sins and those secrets to Him and to someone to whom we are accountable. When we allow the *Son* to expose what is hidden, we can actually see more clearly. The sun can either melt away something, or it can harden it.

How are you going to allow the sun to rise on you today? Will you let the *Son* of God shine on your imperfections?

Prayer: Lord Jesus, I know that I have imperfections in my life. I am scared to show them to You, but I know that shining on them will help me become more like You. Amen.

NOTES

_____

_____

_____

_____

_____

_____

_____

_____

_____

_____

_____

_____

_____

_____

_____

_____

_____

_____

_____

_____

DAY 41

"Rejoice in hope, be patient in tribulation, be constant in prayer."

Romans 12:12

Since patience is a fruit of the spirit, it would be a sour grape. It always looks good, but it is hard to swallow.

My mother softly sang a song about patience to me during my childhood. The song still resounds in my head and heart, especially when our world was in the midst of a pandemic. We did not know when or if it would end. In the beginning, most of us were homebound. Our daughter prayed with such simple faith every day that God would heal the world, and I believed it, too. But when I had to explain to her another day why we could not see our friends, she did not understand why her prayers were not answered immediately.

I think we all want our prayers to be answered immediately. Since we do not see it happen right away, we get sad and disillusioned thinking God did not hear us or does not care about us. In my favorite devotional, *God's Calling*, the most memorable quote is "Delay is not Denial."[6] There are so many times I have reread that day's devotion

---

6   Two Listeners, ibid.

because I need to be reminded that just because we do not hear a yes or no right away does not mean God is not going to answer. The answer could be "not yet."

Are you waiting for a prayer to be answered, a healing to happen, a family member to come to know Jesus, or a financial answer? Right now, even though the season of Lent is coming to an end and many a prayer has yet to be answered, do not give up. The key is to focus on the sacrifice that Christ made for us and to always remember that the answer is on its way.

Prayer: Jesus, You had to wait many years to start Your ministry; and even so, You wanted Your Father's will, rather than Your will to be done. Help me today to not get weary in the waiting. Let me lean on You during this time of "not yet." Thank You for Your example of patience and sacrifice. Amen.

NOTES

_____

_____

_____

_____

_____

_____

_____

_____

_____

_____

DAY 42

"Do not boast about tomorrow, for you do not know what a day may bring."

Proverbs 27:1

There are always going to be surprises in life; it is how we react to them that determines what kind of surprise it will be.

If I was completely honest, I did not have a good day today. I am not sure I handled it well, but the surprise of my life is this continuous battle with Lyme disease and alpha-gal syndrome. I am always surprised by how my body feels—whether it needs a rest day or not. I rested yesterday, since my daughter was at school, so I assumed that I would wake up today feeling better. But I did not.

Before I even got out of bed, my "good" day was out the window. My whole body ached, and anything I did would make me hurt more. Once again, I had to choose to rest. I know I am not suffering as badly as other friends who have Lyme disease and family and friends battling cancer. At the end of the day, all I could do was cry through the frustration because of the pain and the fatigue. I tried my best to use my tired self to pray for others who are suffering more than

I am. Now, do not start thinking I was on my knees all day praying for others; it was mostly a prayer here and a thought there scattered throughout the day.

These surprises of life can be hard to deal with when you have responsibilities that need to be accomplished. Trusting God through these unexpected days is hard, but He does provide just enough strength for what I need to do. Are you facing unexpected trials that interrupt your day? Are you aching in physical or emotional pain that seems to never go away? How are you viewing the unexpected? Thankfully, that day was full of joy watching my little girl dance, play, and sing with so much imagination and freedom. Those are the surprises I want to treasure on this rugged journey. God helped me change my viewpoint of the day.

Prayer: Father God, You know what surprises lie ahead. Please help me know how to handle those surprises and embrace them, even when they do not fit into my plan. Give me the strength to let go of my plan that I hold to tightly and allow Your plan to replace mine. Thank You for Your love and patience as I learn how to let go. Amen.

NOTES

DAY 43

"Brothers, I do not consider that I have made it my own. But one thing I do: forgetting what lies behind and straining forward to what lies ahead."

Philippians 3:13

Speed bumps in life might be failed dreams; they might slow you down, but they do not stop you from moving forward.

I keep hearing the word *failure*. Why are we so afraid of failure? God did not make us all perfect when we were born. He created us with the ability to learn, grow, and mature; but as humans, we still do not like failing. My daughter shows me that regularly. When she is doing new math problems, she expects herself to do it perfectly. I try to encourage her to ask for help, and there are times I need to help her look at that problem differently to solve it.

Jesus' death on the cross looked like a failure to the disciples, but those of us seeing it from this side of the resurrection know that is not true. Is there a failure in your life right now making you doubt that there will be victory on the other side? We need to change our perspective on failure just like I must help my daughter look at her math problems from a different perspective to help complete them. We need to see that resurrection and hope comes from it. When failure knocks you down, let it be a reminder that it is only a speed bump, not a dead end.

Prayer: Jesus, thank You for Your sacrifice and for keeping Your eyes on the path ahead of You, even though others expected something different. Help me recognize that failure is not a setback but can be a "set forward." Show me how to turn my failure around in my life. Amen.

NOTES

_____

_____

_____

_____

_____

_____

_____

_____

_____

_____

_____

_____

_____

_____

_____

DAY 44

"The LORD is near the brokenhearted and saves the crushed in spirit."

Psalm 34:18

*The disciples anticipated great things from Jesus but did not know
that from great pain comes great victory!*

One year, my husband got a little extra in his paycheck, and I asked if we could buy an infrared mat. I had been hearing from other Lyme patients that it really helps with their chronic pain. What I did not know is that it is not a normal heating mat. It says it can penetrate my internal body temperature at least four to six inches deep. What I have learned is that Lyme bacteria love to live in colder temperatures, which is why my body is usually one or two degrees lower than normal temperature. So, just like fever helps our bodies fight diseases, it is the same with the Lyme bacteria. I need to heat them up to kill them.

My doctor told me that when you start killing off the bacteria, the release of toxins can make you feel sicker. That is why I had to take small doses of medicine to kill them slowly. When I go through bouts of great pain, I do know that it is making me better. Heating up the bacteria can be painful but beneficial in the long run.

The same is true in life; sometimes, we need things to be heated up so that the truth is brought out. We cannot keep our hurts, failures, and struggles buried deep down. They will only just fester and grow stronger and root themselves in our lives. God wants to bring things into His light. The heat from His light will expose the pain but will heal us at the same time.

In the past, my emotional hurts had been stuffed down and ignored. What I thought were dumb feelings were bitterness and hurt that God wanted to heal. He was heating it up so that I would deal with the pain properly. After exposing the truth of the bitterness, it was only then that I experienced true freedom.

Have you experienced past hurts that are hard to let go of? Are you holding onto bitterness from those that have hurt you but have not asked for forgiveness? We all have experienced great pain in our lives, whether physical hurt or emotional danger.

Prayer: Lord, we know that our past cannot always be forgotten, but I know You can heal me from it. Help me see that from great pain comes great victory!

NOTES

_____

_____

_____

_____

_____

_____

_____

DAY 45

*"For this is the will of my Father, that everyone who looks on the Son
and believes in him should have eternal life, and I will raise him up
on the last day.'"*

John 6:40

*For some, Good Friday just looks like death; but for those who believe,
it means life everlasting.*

Before Jesus went to the cross, He spent time praying in a garden full of olive trees. Most olive trees live up to five hundred years, but many of them live well over one thousand. It is not that olive trees never die because their trunks do get hollowed out and branches do die, but the roots that have been so deeply and strongly rooted birth new plants.

The disciples in the garden that night did not realize the extent of what was going to happen to Jesus. Just like the olive trees look dead and gone from above the ground, Jesus appeared dead and gone; but His death was only temporary. Is there a dream in our lives that might look dead from the outside? What if what looks dead is just being prepared to burst forth into new life? How can we cultivate the ground to prepare for the new plant?

Like the olive tree's roots underground are still alive and waiting to regrow a new plant, Jesus' death is never the end of the story but only the beginning of a fresh narrative of God's everlasting life waiting for all of us who believe.

Prayer: Jesus, many times I do not want to consider this a good Friday, but it is only good because it is not the end of the story. Help me know that death is not the end of any story, and new life is always about to spring forth. Amen.

NOTES

_____

_____

_____

_____

_____

_____

_____

_____

_____

_____

_____

_____

_____

DAY 46

"When the perishable puts on the imperishable, and the mortal puts
on immortality, then shall come to pass the saying that is written:
'Death is swallowed up in victory.'"

1 Corinthians 15:54

Like the disciples, we mourn Jesus' death, but unlike the disciples,
we know the end of the story: victory wins over death!

I have many crazy, little fears, but one of them is being in a plane crash. It seems obvious that I am afraid of death, but that is not it. I know where I will go if I die, but my fear is surviving the plane crash. Maybe I have watched too many movies and survival stories, but my fear is that I do not have enough energy or strength to survive.

I wonder what the disciples feared. I can imagine their worst fear of Jesus' dying or leaving them came true that fateful weekend of Passover. Many believed He was going to be an earthly King to the Jews by taking over the Romans. Little did they know that God had a bigger plan for them and all of humankind.

What is going on in your life today that you think is dead and gone forever but, in God's eyes, is not finished? What have you packed away and given up hope will never happen? What if God has a bigger dream than yours?

Prayer: Father God, help me to allow You to bring back life into what looks dead and gone. Help me to see the bigger picture that You have in store for all of us. Amen.

NOTES

_____

_____

_____

_____

_____

_____

_____

_____

_____

_____

_____

_____

_____

_____

_____

_____

_____

_____

_____

DAY 47

"'O death, where is your victory? O death, where is your sting?'"

1 Corinthians 15:55

Today ends Lent, but next is a great beginning of a new season of celebration of freedom and resurrection.

esurrection comes from the two old Latin words: *re* and *surgere*. *Re* means "again,"[7] and *surgere* means "to rise."[8] The base of resurrection means "to rise again."[9] I sit here trying to digest these words because yes, I know that Jesus did rise again and that we have that victory over death. But what if we were the disciples? Would we doubt it? Would we run away? Would we have hoped for a victory?

They had seen Him bring Lazarus back to life; but even then, their shock at an empty tomb was unbelievable, especially for Thomas. He could not believe that Jesus was alive. He needed to touch and feel Him to believe. Right now, I know so many suffering because of

---

7   Merriam-Webster, s.v. "Resurrection," Accessed June 14, 2023, https://www.merriam-webster.com/dictionary/resurrection.
8   "Latin is Simple," s.v. "Surgere." Accessed June 15, 2023. https://www.latin-is-simple.com/en/vocabulary/verb/257/?h=surgere.
9   *Merriam-Webster,* s.v. "Re," Accessed June 14, 2023, https://www.merriam-webster.com/dictionary/re.

family deaths or incurable cancers. How do they have hope? Do they need to see Jesus' scars, too? If their spouse is not raised again from the dead, they know they will see them in Heaven. But what happens between those times? Where is the comfort?

The Holy Spirit needs to show up and prepare our hearts for the future of death. Death is not the end result. We need to stand on that promise! We must trust that healing Power—whether it shows up on earth or happens in Heaven. We will all rise again as a new whole body!

Prayer: Thank You, Jesus, for conquering death! Help me choose to live like my complete healing will always be with You in Heaven and with the new earth!

NOTES

BIBLIOGRAPHY

Batterson, Mark. *In a Pit with a Lion on a Snowy Day: How to Survive and Thrive When Opportunity Roars.* Colorado Springs: Multnomah, 2006.

"How Your Lungs Get the Job Done." American Lung Association. July 20, 2017. https://www.lung.org/blog/how-your-lungs-work.

"Latin is Simple." s.v. "Surgere." Accessed June 15, 2023. https://www.latin-is-simple.com/en/vocabulary/verb/257/?h=surgere.

Merriam-Webster. s.v. "Re." Accessed June 14, 2023. https://www.merriam-webster.com/dictionary/re.

Merriam-Webster. s.v. "Resurrection." Accessed June 14, 2023. https://www.merriam-webster.com/dictionary/resurrection.

Spurgeon, Charles Haddon. "The Heart of Flesh." *Metropolitan Tabernacle Pulpit* 19. Kansas City: The Spurgeon Center, 1873. https://www.spurgeon.org/resource-library/sermons/the-heart-of-flesh/#flipbook.

Two Listeners. *God's Calling.* A.J. Russell, Ed. Pasadena: Hope Publishing House. 2012.

ACKNOWLEDGMENTS

To my husband, I write this almost in tears. The journey of healing for me has been long, and you have forever been by my side. They were rough years mentally, emotionally, and financially; and you have stood by me with the help of God on your side. Thank you for keeping those words "in sickness and in health" true!

To my beautiful ballerina daughter, Allene, you might not remember those rough years—and I barely remember them, too—but what I do remember are the moments God spoke to me about you. He healed you as He promised, and I hope you remember that in your life story. Never forget that God holds you in the palm of His hand and has great plans for you.

To my comedian, Ender, you are the miracle I didn't know would happen. God blessed me by giving me back memories of you that I missed with Allene when she was young. Thank you for bringing so much laughter into our home. You and your sister will wow a lot of crowds in the future!

To my parents, thank you for being brave enough to follow God's calling into one of the most dangerous countries at that time. Thank you for always being generous in love, encouragement, and support to others, no matter where we are. Thank you for coming off the mission field to help me. Thank you for all the miles we drove to

so many doctors. Thank you for being wonderful grandparents.
Remember your rewards for all your sacrifices are in Heaven.

About the Author

Chelsea grew up as a missionary kid in Bogota, Colombia, and Quito, Ecuador. After college, she moved to Bangkok, Thailand, as a missionary for two years besides working various jobs and moving around from Florida to Missouri to North Carolina until she met her husband on a missionary kid retreat in Spain. They live in Centerton, Arkansas, with their two kids and are still involved in their local church and helping missionary kids when they can.

Contact Information

C.J. Vegter can be contacted by email:

chelseajvegter@gmail.com

Also via these social media sites and website:

Website/blog address: www.cjvegter.com

Facebook: www.facebook.com/cjvegter

Instagram: www.instagram.com/cjvegter

Podcast: https://podcasters.spotify.com/pod/show/ chelsea-j-vegter

Ambassador International's mission is to magnify the Lord Jesus Christ and promote His Gospel through the written word.

We believe through the publication of Christian literature, Jesus Christ and His Word will be exalted, believers will be strengthened in their walk with Him, and the lost will be directed to Jesus Christ as the only way of salvation.

For more information about
AMBASSADOR INTERNATIONAL
please visit:

www.ambassador-international.com
@AmbassadorIntl
www.facebook.com/AmbassadorIntl

Thank you for reading this book!

You make it possible for us to fulfill our mission, and we are grateful for your partnership.

To help further our mission, please consider leaving us a review on your social media, favorite retailer's website, Goodreads or Bookbub, or our website.

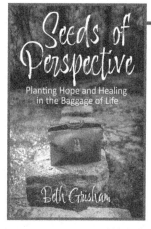

In *Seeds of Perspective*, women of all ages and walks of life willingly poured out their most difficult life situations as a personal sacrifice to help others process and find hope and healing in their own worst mistakes. They believe that remembering and sharing their stories awakens in each of us a deeper understanding of God's promise to redeem our lives for His glory and His purposes and to bring beauty from the ashes of our past.

How do you think God feels about you? Take a moment for the honest truth. Let the soul-searching question seep in, and brace yourself for the answer. Like treasure left too long, they're buried in the Bible but finally brought to light in "Always Been Loved." As you read it, you'll finally discover God's true feelings for you—the feelings He's had for you since before you were born and that you can never lose. He's ready to show you: you've always been loved.

What does it mean to really live? Using Jesus' Sermon on the Mount as the blueprint, Martin Wiles answers some of the most pressing questions Christians have about effective Christian living. In this powerful work, Martin shares eighteen insights for learning how to pray, handle our anger, love our enemies, overcome worry, have a healthy marriage, and so much more. *Don't Just Live … Really Live* offers a practical approach for discerning how to live out the Bible in today's world.